IMAGES OF ENGLAND

ROCHESTER

IMAGES OF ENGLAND

ROCHESTER

ALAN MOSS AND BOB RATCLIFFE

The
History
Press

Frontispiece: There are many faces from yesteryear, carved in stone and wood, watching over today's visitors to Rochester. Green men abound in the cathedral, some of the oldest dating from the fourteenth century. The most impressive of these form the bosses to the ceiling of the nave crossing and were restored in 1840.

First published 2006

Reprinted 2013

The History Press
The Mill, Brimscombe Port,
Stroud, Gloucestershire, GL5 2QG
www.thehistorypress.co.uk

British Library Cataloguing in Publication Data.
A catalogue record for this book is available from the British Library.

ISBN 978 0 7524 3840 5

Typesetting and origination by
Tempus Publishing Limited.
Printed and bound in Great Britain by
Marston Book Services Limited, Didcot

Contents

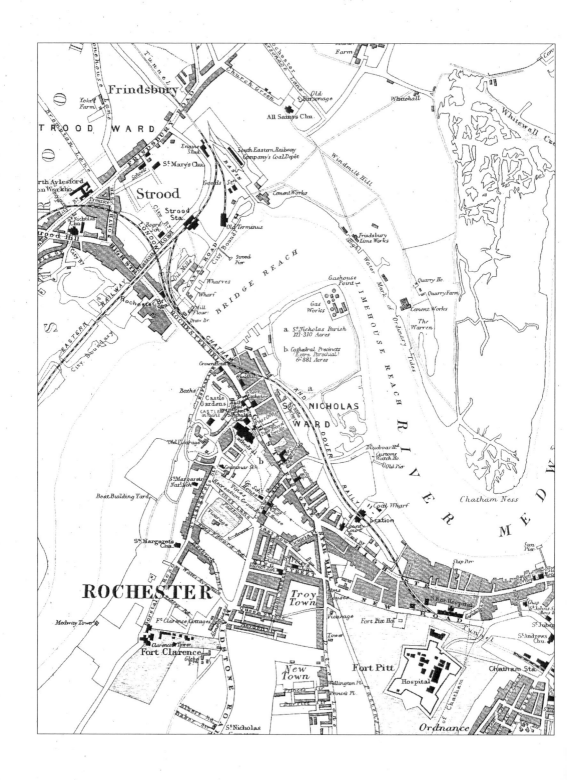

Acknowledgements

Our thanks go to the following, all of whom who have either allowed us to use material from their collections or have given us valuable assistance in our research; they are: Norma Crowe and Janet Knight, of Medway Archives and Local Studies Centre; the Dean and Chapter of Rochester Cathedral; the Dudley Studios Collection; Bernard Snell of Fine Art Studios; the Locomotive Club of Great Britain; Geoff Matthews and Kevin Russell. Our thanks also go to the many anonymous photographers of a bygone age without whose efforts the production of this book would not have been possible.

Introduction

Over the years much has been written about Rochester and this book does not attempt to be a detailed history of the area. Rather, it comprises a number of sections illustrating specific parts of the area through the use of photographs accompanied by extended captions.

It has been said that one picture is worth a thousand words and we hope that these 192 illustrations will do much to aid today's historian in his or her study of Rochester, as well as bring back past memories to our long-term residents. Such are two objectives of this book, but it also has another objective: that of ensuring the illustrations survive. Old photographs and their negatives are notoriously fragile and can easily be lost. The glass plate negatives of the past were easily broken or damaged. Exposure to the damp, for example, could result in the emulsion floating off. A print from one such damaged plate is included in this book, on p.116. It is the only known photograph of the High Street frontage of Eastgate House before the 1897 restoration, and for that reason is unique and worthy of reproduction, even though the top left-hand corner has been lost. This particular photograph was taken by a doctor from Faversham, whose glass plate negatives were rescued from a derelict garage in that town in 1955. They were nearly lost for ever, but today they make a fascinating archive of an amateur photographer of the 1890s. Sadly, such a happy ending to the tale is not always the case, and whole collections have been accidentally or wantonly lost. A local example of a such a loss was the clearance of an entire cellar full of glass plate negatives. It was 'skipped' by the new non-photographic owner of the property, which had been the home of a major photographic studio.

The sources that constitute the photographs that illustrate this book are many and varied. Some are from postcards taken by cameramen working for national companies, while others are from local amateur and professional photographers. The latter group includes some from the portfolio of the late Phil Towner of Dudley Studios, whose casual shots of traffic jams in the 1950s are real gems that could so easily have passed unrecorded. The everyday street scene and, in particular, its traffic, is rarely taken. The photographer usually waits for a break in the traffic to capture his or her subject but it is the very traffic that they have been striving to avoid that will often be the item of greatest interest. In a similar vein there are countless photographs of the cathedral, both before and after the spire was added in 1904, but there is only one known view of the spire when it was under construction - and that was taken more by accident than design (see p.14). Others were surely taken, but they have yet to come to light.

The source of some of our illustrations is known, and is duly acknowledged. We have been unable to ascertain the identity of the majority of the photographers themselves, but we do thank those ladies and gentlemen of a bygone age, whose photographic equipment was considerably more weighty than today's digital camera and without whom such a book as this would have been impossible to produce.

In conclusion, we make a plea to you, dear reader. If you have any old photographs or negatives of the local area that might be of interest to others, please do not let them end their days in a bin or on a rubbish tip. Show them in the first instance to the people of the Medway Archives and Local Studies Centre in Strood. There is little chance of financial remuneration but your old photo may, just may, fill in a part of the jigsaw that is the ongoing tale of Rochester and the Medway and it could one day even appear in a book just like this one. It is only by the production of topographical books such as this that old photographs can be assured of a future in the entertainment and education of generations to come.

Alan Moss and Bob Ratcliffe
Rochester, 2006

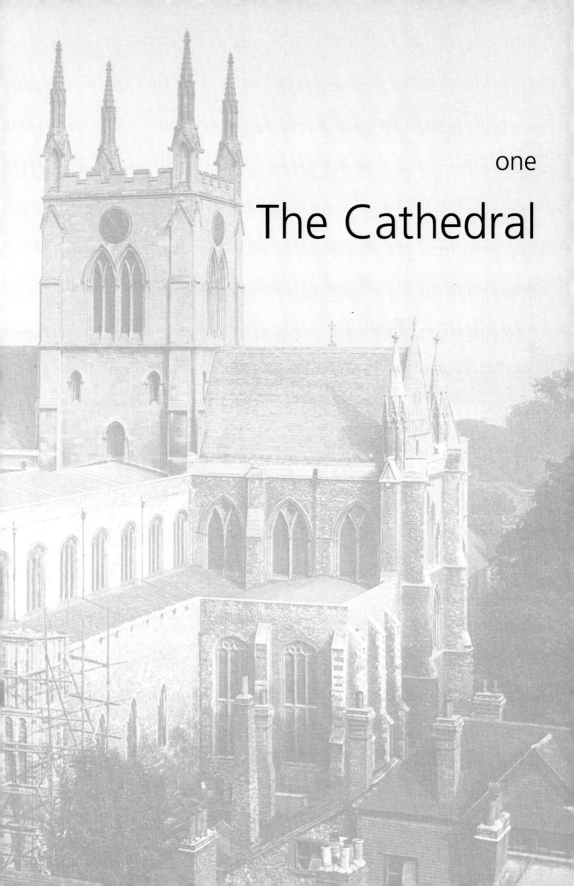

one

The Cathedral

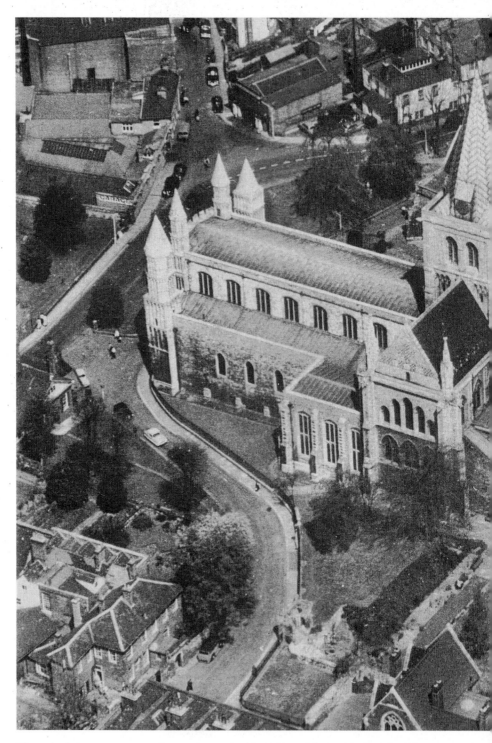

The cathedral presents an amazing roof-scape in this 1960s aerial view. To the left of the tower the lead roofs cover the oldest part of the building, which is the twelfth century nave and aisles that had a clerestory added in 1430. To the right of the tower the slate roof of the

ER CATHEDRAL

31261

nineteenth century covers the thirteenth-century choir. The buildings in the top left-hand corner, which include the former police station, were demolished in 1975.

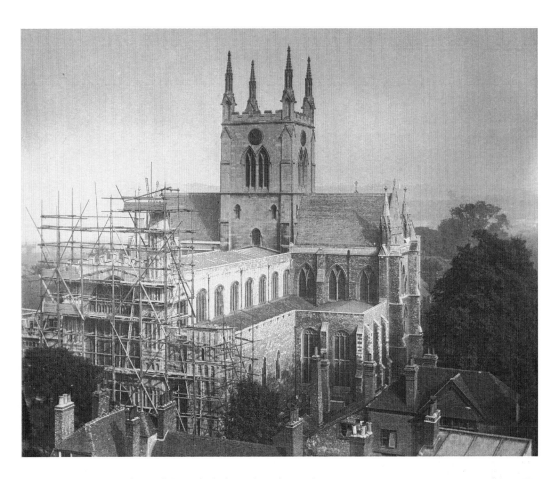

Above: The west front of the cathedral was the subject of a restoration in 1894 under John Loughborough Pearson, when the three missing turrets were rebuilt. It was to be a further ten years before Charles Hodgson Fowler rebuilt the tower and incorporated a new spire, a replica of that of the fourteenth century that had been removed by Louis Cottingham, in 1825.

Right: With the completion of the new spire in 1904, the cathedral looked much as it does today, over a century later, though the foreground presents an entirely different aspect.

Opposite: The cathedral and its precinct were originally enclosed by walls, with gates at the points of access – three of which survive today. Access from Boley Hill to the west end was only available to pedestrians when this photograph was taken, c. 1890.

Above: This postcard of Prior's Gate is the only known record of the cathedral's present spire being built in 1904. It is amazing that such a major alteration to Rochester's skyline was not better recorded.

Left: The area to the south of the cathedral is known as The Precincts, and most of the property here is owned by the Dean and Chapter or by King's School. It was here that the monastic buildings stood from the foundation of the Benedictine priory in 1077 until its dissolution at the reformation in 1542.

Opposite above and below: In 1805 a canon's house was built in the area of the cloisters, together with a coach house and stables at the corner of Minor Canon Row. For 135 years it precluded access to the cloisters and spoiled the view of the south side of the choir. It is seen above in an early twentieth century view from Prior's Gate. In 1937 this house was demolished and the area of the cloisters returned to public use. In the view from an upper window in Minor Canon Row (*below*), demolition work is well under way. In the foreground, the area of the coach house will soon become an enclosed garden. The gate in the wall, in the extreme left background, is today all that remains as evidence that a house once stood here.

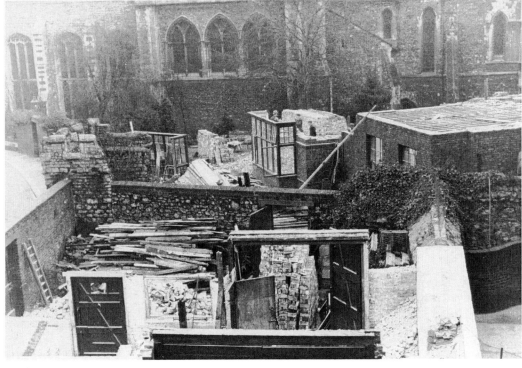

Choir Screen, Rochester Cathedral

Above: The wall between the nave and the choir was a very plain affair until 1877 when it was used as the base for a richly decorated memorial to Dean Scott. The eight figures represent important men in the history of the cathedral. They include its founder (in AD 604) St Justus; Gundulph, our Norman builder bishop; and John Fisher, bishop here until his martyrdom in 1535.

Right: In most churches the font is to be found near the main entrance. The font in the cathedral, sculpted by Thomas Earp, is a fine example of Victorian worksmanship and a memorial to Canon H.W. Burrows, who served from 1881-1892. It once stood in the centre of the nave, as seen here, but today has been re-sited under the Norman arcade on the south side, near the west door.

Opposite: The main arcade and the triforium of the nave are late Norman work, dating from the early twelfth century, while the clerestory and roof were replaced in 1430. The Norman work is seen to advantage in this elevated view from the sill of the west window.

FONT, ROCHESTER CATHEDRAL.

Left: A gem inside the cathedral is the fourteenth century doorway into the library. Known as the Chapter House Doorway, the carving represents the new Christian church on the left and the old religion on the right. Very similar figures may be seen in Strasbourg Cathedral.

Below: The bell tower contains a frame of ten bells, seen here at bell founders Gillett and Johnson's yard in 1921. The bells are regularly rung on Sunday mornings, with practice on Thursday evenings, as well as for weddings and other special occasions.

two

The Castle

CITY OF  ROCHESTER.

PURCHASE OF THE CASTLE GARDENS.

ORDER AND ROUTE OF THE

PROCESSION

24th OCTOBER, 1883.

The Procession will start from the Guildhall at half-past One o'clock in the following order:---

Fife and Drum Band.

The 8th and 9th Batteries of the 1st Kent Artillery Volunteers.

The Rochester Volunteer Fire Brigade.

The Superintendent of Police and the City Police Force.

The Acting Principal Sergeant-at-Mace.

The Under Sergeants-at-Mace.

The Chamberlain of the Rochester Oyster Fishery.

The Mayor.

The Aldermen.

The Town Clerk. The Clerk of the Peace.

The Justices' Clerk. The City Treasurer.

The Deputy Coroner.

The Councillors.

The Citizens and Friends.

The Procession will proceed *via* the High Street, King's Head Lane, and Castle Hill, through the Gardens to the Band Stand, and return through the Esplanade Entrance along the Esplanade and High Street to the Corn Exchange.

By order,

RICHARD PRALL,
TOWN CLERK.

EDWIN HARRIS AND SON, PRINTERS, 89, EASTGATE, ROCHESTER.

Above: The castle looms over the trees in this late nineteenth-century view. The area where the photographer is standing is one which had only just been cleared of buildings, allowing the road to the right - Boley Hill - to be widened to ease the passage of vehicles out of the city. The railed area in the middle distance is part of the old cathedral graveyard.

Right: Over the centuries many houses were built close to the city and castle walls and many a garden flourished in the shelter afforded by them. This charming view shows the garden of one of the houses which stood in Boley Hill, nestling under the castle walls. The clearance of these houses in the 1950s created the open space and magnificent view of the castle which we enjoy today.

Cathedral, Jubilee Memorial and Castle, Rochester.

THE CASTLE, ROCHESTER

Above and opposite: These three views of the castle gardens, taken over a period of about fifty years, chart the sad fate of the memorial which was erected to commemorate Queen Victoria's Golden Jubilee in 1887. The delicate design of the monument and the softness of the stone from which it was made gave it a comparatively short life. By the end of the Second World War almost all trace of it had gone. Other disappearing features include the railings around the memorial, as well as trees nearby. Preparations for the great historical Pageant held here in 1931 included the creation of a large open space for the arena and grandstands, which robbed the gardens of many fine trees and bushes. The railings succumbed to the scrap metal drive of 1940.

Prior to the demolition of the medieval bridge in 1856, the waters of the Medway had lapped against the western wall of the castle. Some of the rubble from that bridge was used to build up the foreshore and create the Esplanade. The wide gap in the wall at this point was the result of the quarrying of the stone for other buildings, including Upnor Castle further downstream. Notice the scales and other slot machines on the left.

In 1906 a new retaining wall was constructed, above which terraces were created giving fine views of the river. Seats were provided both on the terraces and in the alcoves, the latter being a haven for courting couples! The number of people in the picture is an indication of how popular the Esplanade was for promenading and taking the air, before more sophisticated pleasures came to occupy our time. In the right background can be seen the building which housed swimming and slipper baths, provided at the expense of the Richard Watts charity.

Right: The castle gardens have always been a popular venue for entertainment, especially music. This handbill from 1883 advertises a concert by the band of the 2nd Battalion of the East Lancashire Regiment. The castle's musical tradition is today upheld by an annual season of summer evening concerts which attract many thousands of people.

Below: Having taken a lease on the castle estate from the Earl of Jersey in 1870, the council lost no time in turning the grounds into a public amenity. In the best municipal traditions of the nineteenth century, a bandstand was erected, the corner stone being laid by the mayor, John Ross Foord, on 18 October 1871. Sadly, only the stone base now remains.

CASTLE GARDENS.

Saturday Evenings for the People.

BAND
2ND BATTALION
EAST LANCASHIRE REGT.

PROGRAMME.

1. OVERTURE ...."Zampa" .... *Herold*
2. MAZURKA........."Augusta" .. ..*Parlon*
3. SELECTION.."Les Cloches de Corneville" ....*Planquette*
4. VALSE ......"Ehren on the Rhine" ......*Hutchison*
5. FANTASIA......"Songs of Wales" .... *Vanchaanen*
6. GALOP........ "Who goes there"...........*Meissler*

"God save the Queen."

Conductor, T. GORDON,

BANDMASTER.

Edwin Harris and Son, Printers. 89, Eastgate, Rochester.

Castle Gardens Rochester.
Feeding the Pigeons.

Whilst the purist might regret the pillaging of the old curtain wall for its reusable stone, the creation of the terraces in the resultant gap proved to be an instant hit with visitors to the castle gardens. West facing, they take full advantage of the afternoon sun. To the left of this view can be seen the fine array of trees and shrubs with which the gardens were adorned in their early days. Most were removed in 1931 to make way for the Pageant.

Today both the castle and the cathedral are impressively floodlit after dark, a fact which is taken for granted in this hitech age. In earlier days, however, floodlighting would have been attempted only to mark special occasions or events. Here, the keep stands out brightly against the darkened sky when it was illuminated as part of the celebrations surrounding the 1931 Pageant.

three

The Two
High Streets

St Margaret's Banks, or simply The Banks, is a narrow road which runs for several hundred yards parallel to, but at a higher level than, the east end of Rochester High Street. It recalls a time, before the coming of the railway and riverside industry replaced the marshes, when the tide might flood right up to this point. This early twentieth-century view shows a stretch of The Banks typically crammed with shops and other small businesses.

After the Second World War The Banks became something of a commercial backwater and went into a gradual decline from which it never fully recovered. Piecemeal demolition and redevelopment later robbed it of much of its charm and character. However, the area has recently undergone something of a revival, with new housing replacing the run-down buildings on the left.

The advertisement in the bottom left-hand corner for the latest production at the Theatre Royal dates this picture at least to the early 1880s. Here, Star Hill descends towards its junction with the High Street. Straight ahead takes the traveller towards the bridge and to the right the High Street heads back towards Chatham. Most of the buildings in this picture have since been demolished. Only the tall shops in the centre would be recognisable today. The Theatre Royal, which was patronised by Charles Dickens, closed its doors for the last time in 1884. A photograph of the Theatre Royal may be seen on p.125.

All the buildings in the foreground of this 1920s view would soon be demolished to enable the junction of Star Hill (right) and High Street to be widened. The high gables in the background provide a glimpse of the future street scene. In the shop to the left of the Star Hotel a 'rebuilding sale' is under way, while on the extreme right the new Star Hotel rises behind scaffolding. A lull in the traffic gives the policeman on point duty a chance to rest his arms.

Most of the buildings seen here were demolished in 1902 to make way for Mr Franklin Homan's new furniture store, subsequently the showroom and offices of the Kent Electric Power Co. and later still of the South Eastern Electricity Board. J.T. Ogden continued to trade from this and other premises in the High Street until the 1970s. The town pump dates from 1763; it is now preserved at the guildhall museum. A note on the back of the postcard tells us that the gentleman standing in Ogden's doorway is Mr Alfred Cole of Union Street.

The driver of the car approaching the camera is cautiously avoiding the tramlines by the expedience of driving up the middle of the road! He had little to worry about as motor traffic was still relatively light in this picture from the 1920s. Edwin Smith is advertising Whitbread's ales and stout at his shop on the extreme right – a shop which remains an off-licence today.

'A street of gables' was how Rochester High Street was once described. Some still remain and the fine range of buildings in the centre is little changed today. Charles Dickens chose it as the setting for Mr Pumblechook's corn chandlery in *Great Expectations*. The young hero, Pip, was lodged here on the night before going to the guildhall to be sworn in as an apprentice to Joe Gargery, the blacksmith.

A lady makes a mental note of the latest additions to Mr Seeley's drapery display as she hurries past 154 High Street. Subsequent changes of ownership mean that one now wines and dines where, in the early decades of the twentieth century, the ladies of the city purchased their ribbons and linen. The presence of the photographer goes unnoticed except by two of the children standing by the handcart.

Above: This scene has almost completely changed since this picture was taken around the turn of the twentieth century. Sir Joseph Williamson's Mathematical School, the little greengrocery shop (which also served as the school tuck shop) and, on the extreme right, the Blue Boar public house, are now but fading memories. The entire site is now covered by the city's main car park. Other pictures of the Mathematical School are on pages 108 and 109.

Left: Free School Lane led down from the High Street, between the Mathematical School and Mrs Hubbard's shop, to Corporation Street (formerly The Common). In the distance can be seen the maltings which once stood at the end of the lane. The presence of tram lines and the little motor van suggest a date for this picture of sometime during the 1920s.

Here, the presence of the photographer has attracted some youthful attention. Indeed, the young man on the left seems intent on getting in the picture. The name Leonards appears on a shop on the left. This recalls a 'high class' ladies' outfitter and linen drapery which traded in the High Street for many decades - the sort of shop which has now all but disappeared from most town centres.

Buses have replaced trams in this post-1930 view of the High Street. On the extreme right is the Poor Travellers' House, of Richard Watts' charity, while next door is the headquarters of the Rochester, Chatham and Gillingham Gas Co.. In appearance, the Poor Travellers' House remains unchanged to this day. Soon after this picture was taken, however, the gas company replaced their premises with an imposing new building which now houses the city's visitor information centre.

It is 22 June 1911 and decorations abound in the High Street in honour of King George V's coronation. The presence in the picture of military personnel - most of whom seem to be heading back towards Chatham and the barracks - suggests that they may have attended official celebrations in the cathedral. Many of the buildings seen here are recognisable today, although the shop with the attractive wrought-iron balcony has been replaced with a new building.

Opposite above and below: Two very different views of Chertsey's Gate, but separated by only a few years. The gate once gave, or withheld, access from the High Street to the cathedral and (until 1540) to St Andrew's Priory. In the first view *(right)*, there is still a sense of the separation once enjoyed by the monks. The second view *(below)*, however, shows how the scene had changed by 1903. Mr Chalmers' hardware shop had been demolished, Boley Hill had been widened at its junction with the High Street, and Chertsey's Gate had lost its role as the main thoroughfare to the cathedral. A fortunate side effect of the work was the opening up of a fine view of the castle keep.

The opening up of the junction between the High Street and Boley Hill afforded better access to the south of the city and, via St Margaret's Street, to the villages along the Medway towards Maidstone. Here, a carrier's cart from one of the outlying villages emerges from Boley Hill into the High Street as a tram passes on its way to Frindsbury.

Crowds have gathered on this usually quiet stretch of the High Street, creating problems for the drivers of the passing trams. The presence of an army officer in a plumed helmet suggests that the crowds have been attracted there by an event of some significance, perhaps a military parade. The buildings facing the camera in the distance were to be demolished in the 1960s to make way for the approach to the new Rochester Bridge.

The angle of the sun and the time on the corn exchange clock suggest it is early evening, which makes the absence of traffic in the High Street all the more remarkable, even if this picture was taken soon after the Second World War. The city restaurant - erected in 1903 - was, in reality, a public house. It still stands, although no longer as a public house. It is an Italian restaurant at the time of writing. The traffic lights have gone; they were made redundant in the 1970s when the High Street ceased to be part of the A2 trunk road. Gone too is the police telephone box on the street corner. It recalls an era before portable radios and telephones.

A 'demented chapel' was how Charles Dickens once described the Rochester Corn Exchange. Financed by Admiral Sir Cloudesley Shovell MP in 1706, the building was conceived as the gatehouse to the butchers', and later to the corn chandlers', markets. The bell in the cupola was the signal for the start and finish of trading. The market buildings have long gone, replaced by two assembly rooms. One is the Prince's Hall and the other, with its main entrance in Northgate, is now known as the Queen's Hall. The former served as Rochester's first cinema from 1910 to 1924.

The guildhall weathervane towers over all and the Duke's Head still stands next to the guildhall in this photograph taken towards the end of the nineteenth century. The lamp and pillar on the extreme left marked the start of the 1856 bridge, which is behind the photographer. Within a few years, many of the buildings on the left would be demolished to make way for Corporation Street, a relief road of the High Street, though the Gundulph public house was to remain until yet further road widening took place in 1968.

The approach to the new bridge of 1856 is in the foreground of this view of the Crown Hotel, the four gables of which front onto the High Street. This lovely medieval timber-framed building was to be swept away in 1863 and replaced with the present Crown. The name of the adjoining public house, City Arms, was transferred to new premises in Victoria Street.

Above and below: A short walk across Rochester Bridge brings the traveller into Strood and into the city's other High Street. Until real improvements were made to the drainage system in the mid-twentieth century, flooding was an ever-present threat here. On 1 November 1921, the photographer has clambered up on to the railway bridge to record the unhappy scene. On the right of the picture, the watery theme is continued in the advertisement for Messrs Dove, Phillips & Pett's mineral waters which were manufactured nearby. Meanwhile, in the same location a car appears to have been abandoned across the junction of High Street and Station Road, the impasse giving the passengers on the tram ample time to take note of the latest production at Chatham's Empire Theatre. A train of wagons belonging to the South Eastern and Chatham Railway trundles along the Maidstone line, overhead.

During the first half of the twentieth century, Strood High Street lost most of its quaint old shops and houses in a succession of piecemeal redevelopment schemes. The open space on the right would later be developed, with a new parade of shops and the Invicta Cinema. By the end of the 1960s nearly all the buildings on the left would be demolished. Some would be replaced by more modern buildings, but the site of those nearest to the camera would be covered by tarmac as part of a scheme aimed at easing the city's traffic congestion.

Above and below: Two views of Strood High Street in the 1960s as work was getting under way on the road-widening scheme. The hardware shop on the extreme right of the top picture - of which there were a number of branches in Kent - bore the unusual name of Mence Smith. In the lower picture the approaching bus is on the Maidstone and District company's No. 57 route from Gravesend to Hastings.

STROOD HIGH STREET.

(East Side) from Station
Road, 1906. 43

The Strood Turnpike, or toll gate, stood at the junction of the High Street and Cage Lane (now North Street). It was removed on 1 December 1876, the day on which this photograph was taken. The toll payable for a coach drawn by six horses in 1792 was one shilling, making it a very expensive way of travelling indeed. On the extreme right of the picture is the Angel public house. There has been an Angel inn hereabouts for at least 400 years and this road junction, although entirely changed, today retains the name Angel Corner. The latest version of the Angel stands nearby.

Opposite above and below: A series of official photographs of the centre of the city was taken prior to the construction of the tramway, including these two of Strood High Street. The top picture shows the International Stores, a familiar feature of most high streets until it succumbed to the supermarkets in the 1970s. The lower picture shows the High Street near its junction with Station Road. All the buildings to the left of the railway bridge appear run down and empty. They would shortly be replaced by new shops and the Invicta Cinema (see also p.40).

The same location as in the picture on p.43, this time at about the turn of the twentieth century, and looking towards Rochester Bridge. The sparse traffic, even for those far off days, belies the fact that this was the main road from Dover and Canterbury to London.

A few steps back and some thirty years on in time finds a very different view of almost the same location. It can be dated to the early 1930s: the tram lines were removed after closure of the system in 1930, but the hoarding in North Street is still advertising Barnard's Palace of Varieties in Chatham, which was destroyed by fire in 1934. The policeman on point duty has little to disturb him in this tranquil scene. H.C. Hill & Son, well-known fishmongers and poulterers, continued to trade on the High Street until well after the Second World War.

four

Retail Trade

GEORGE J. JENKINS, FISHMONGER, POULTERER AND LICENSED DEALER IN GAME, HIGH ST., ROCHESTER.

Above: Mr Jenkins had an advertising card produced to spread the word of his wares, which could be delivered throughout the city. His shop was next door to another of the lost inns of Rochester, the Royal Life Boat, which was demolished around 1910 and rebuilt as a shop.

Left: Number 151 High Street was the home of Edwin Harris's printing works, from which countless leaflets and posters came, recording the history and activities of the area. Harris was a keen Dickensian and local guide. He also wrote a number of 'historic novels', the accent being more on the novel than the historic element.

Above: Leonard's department store developed in piecemeal fashion from Nos 108 to 118 High Street, resulting in a somewhat chaotic internal layout. Externally, the original street elevations could still be ascertained from the line of upper floors. The name boards had incised serif lettering carved in timber and were gilded, being faced with 6mm of plate glass. Leonard's was a popular store and its abrupt closure in 1968 was greatly lamented. The site has since been redeveloped.

Right: The High Street has always boasted a number of specialist shops, including at one time Mr Brignall's Bed Manufactory. What would Mr Brignall have thought of a more recent retailer specialising in water beds?

Above: Robert Dale & Son offered a wide range of groceries at their Castle Stores in the High Street, established in 1885, where the aroma of freshly-ground coffee wafting in the air was a great attraction. In 1929 the staff lined up for a photograph with the then owner, Mr R. Martin Dale, who is on the left.

Left: Bargains were always to be had at J.H. Thomas's auction rooms at 186 High Street, next door to Berkeley House. In the days before MFI, good quality second-hand furniture was the usual way to set up home.

Opposite above and below: Two pictures of the premises of the Rochester and District Co-operative Society. The main city store *(above)* was at 25 High Street, Rochester, while the second branch *(below)* was at 123 Delce Road. Those were the days when it was perfectly acceptable to have joints of meat hanging out in the open air and when window dressing was an acquired art. Note the biscuit tins in the doorway. These would be collectors' items today.

The Co-op ran a fine drapery and millinery department as part of their High Street store. George Lane is to the right of this view of a very well-dressed window. This part of the store later became the grocery department and included a post office counter. The Co-op transferred their main retail operation across the river to Strood High Street when the latter was redeveloped in the 1960s.

Almost every street corner had its own grocery, greengrocery or tobacconist's shop in the days before supermarkets. They served the needs of those for whom, without car or refrigerator, shopping was a daily necessity, and flourished when the ban on tobacco advertising was clearly still a long way off. Mr Munton's Tuck Shop was at the corner of Cossack Street and Rose Street.

Horsnaill and Reynolds, corn merchants, occupied Nos 57 and 58 High Street, Strood, where a likely lad has just purchased a new bin. Or has he? Most likely the picture has been carefully posed. At any rate, the detail of the nineteenth-century shopfront, with its slender mullions and panelled stall board, is well recorded. Note also the corn painted on the rendered first-floor frontage.

Once a separate village overlooking Rochester from the high ground to the north, Frindsbury had, by the twentieth century, become part of the city, physically if not yet administratively. This photograph, taken in the second decade of the century, shows some of the small shops which served the everyday needs of its people. Subsequent road widening has swept away nearly all the buildings in this scene.

IRONMONGER LANE.
(Eastgate End) now
Corporation Street.

1903 Act.

Ironmonger Lane became part of Corporation Street (which was subsequently part of the A2 trunk road) after improvements were carried out under an Act of Parliament passed in 1903. The Red Lion (right) was rebuilt at this time, but Clift's, jewellers and pawnbrokers, survived until a further road-widening scheme in the 1980s. A full picture of the Red Lion can be found on p.83.

This very early, if rather poor quality, view of the High Street from Chertsey's Gate records a number of buildings which are long gone. The shop nearest the camera stood at the corner of Pump Lane and was demolished in 1895 to enable the lane to be widened and transformed into Northgate. By that time the two small weatherboarded shops adjoining it had also been replaced by what, in 2006, is Slinder's, a florist.

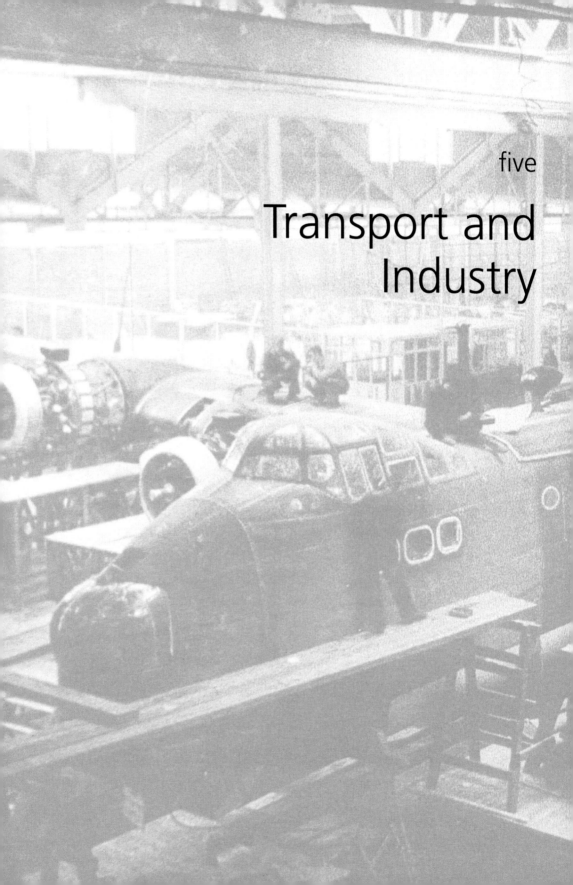

five

Transport and
Industry

Rochester Bridge, *c.*1840. This fine print shows the fourteenth-century bridge in its final form, just before its demolition. Although of graceful proportions, it had become inadequate for the traffic which by then was passing over and beneath it. During demolition some of the balustrade was removed and placed along the esplanade, where it can still be seen today.

Opposite above: The old and the new bridges are here seen in 1856. The new structure, designed by Sir William Cubitt, is open and the old bridge has been closed to traffic and awaits its fate. The new bridge sits on the alignment of its Roman forebear, enabling traffic to pass in a straight line between the city's two High Streets (of Rochester and Strood) without the awkward twists and turns necessitated by the old bridge. The plate girders on the right form the railway bridge of the East Kent Railway, to be opened in 1858.

Opposite below: Work was well advanced on the new bridge when the photographer captured this family group posing on Strood Esplanade. The fifty-foot western-most span, seen in the centre of the picture, was designed to be swung open to allow for the passage of ships. In the event this facility was never used. The bridge was opened, amid much public rejoicing, by the mayors and aldermen of Rochester and Maidstone on 13 August 1856.

On 16 February 1913 the passengers on a Chatham and District tram get a close-up view of the work which transformed the appearance of Rochester Bridge and which allowed the removal of Cubitt's graceful, if hazardous, arches. The work also included raising the deck by six feet. The remodelled bridge was declared open by the Countess of Darnley on 14 May 1914.

Opposite above: Sir William Cubitt had offered the bridge wardens a number of designs, including one for a suspension bridge. The final design, of a cast iron bridge of three arches with an opening span, was influenced by the wishes of the Admiralty. Here, maintenance or repair work is going on beneath the bridge deck. The parallel railway bridge, opened in 1858, can just be glimpsed on the extreme left of the picture.

Opposite below: The 1856 bridge had a relatively short life. Trade on the river was brisk at this time, with many vessels passing through the relatively low arches of the bridge every day. Collisions occurred, resulting, as in this picture, in quite serious damage to the bridge. The problem was solved in 1912 by a major rebuild which gave more headroom to passing ships.

A fire-fighting tug tackles a serious fire on the former South Eastern Railway bridge in June 1919. The bridge was closed and rail traffic between Strood and Rochester transferred to the adjoining bridge which then carried the London, Chatham and Dover main line. Following a later rationalisation of the tracks, all trains now use the SER bridge, the former LCDR bridge having been rebuilt for road traffic in the 1960s.

This 1930s view shows the remodelled road bridge and the two parallel railway bridges, the nearer of which was built by the East Kent Railway (later to become the London, Chatham and Dover Railway) in 1858 and the further by the South Eastern Railway, in 1890. Drivers on the road bridge are warned of a speed limit of eight miles per hour for any vehicle weighing over twenty tons, and an absolute limit of thirty tons.

Above and right: Here, in 1857, work is in progress to demolish the medieval bridge. The white building in the centre of the picture is the Bridge Chamber, the office of Rochester Bridge Trust. Its rebuilding in the 1870s revealed the remains of the fourteenth-century chapel of All Souls *(right)*, which had been concealed behind the later façade. The chapel remained in this ruinous state until 1937 when, after a lengthy debate with the Charity Commission, the Bridge Trust were allowed to apply money from their funds to its restoration. It was re-roofed and furnished and now serves as a meeting room for the Trust.

The winter of 1895/96 was a hard one. The river froze over, bringing traffic to a halt. You can feel the cold of this misty morning, with the collier *City of Rochester* and numerous barges lying amid the ice floes off Blue Boar Pier. Three of them at least were still tiller-steered, in the days before the introduction of wheels eased the bargee's burden.

The red hulls of Johan Lauritzen's Danish fleet were a common sight at Blue Boar Pier in the 1950s, exemplified here by the *Fenja Dan*. Her cargo of wood pulp is being discharged into lighters for onward transit up the Medway to the paper mills of A.E. Reed at New Hythe.

1932 saw the arrival of the barque *Peking* which had been purchased by the Shaftsbury Foundation as a replacement for their training ship *Arethusa*. *Peking* was converted at Acorn shipyard and renamed *Arethusa* after her predecessor, before becoming a part of the river scene at Upnor until 1975.

Bridge Reach was the furthest point upriver accessible for ships with fixed masts, three of which can be seen in this 1900 view. There are also no fewer than twenty-four barges, and the paddle steamer *Princess of Wales* is on the left, heading for Southend. The jetty in the foreground was the chalk wharf, where empty ships could load chalk as ballast before leaving the river.

Bridge Reach from Frindsbury, with the castle and cathedral in the distance. A three-masted sailing vessel lies off Strood Pier, discharging her cargo into lighters, while a 'stumpie' barge (a barge with a main mast but no top mast) lies at a buoy on the left. Careful study of the bridge shows the under-road arches of the 1856 bridge, with one span of the over-road replacement in position on the Strood side, thus dating the view at 1912. Chalk quarrying later removed the field behind the fence in the foreground.

Barge building was a fairly basic craft undertaken with the minimum of facilities. The beginnings of another Sailorman can be seen here 'in frame' in a well-ventilated shed in Canal Road, around 1880.

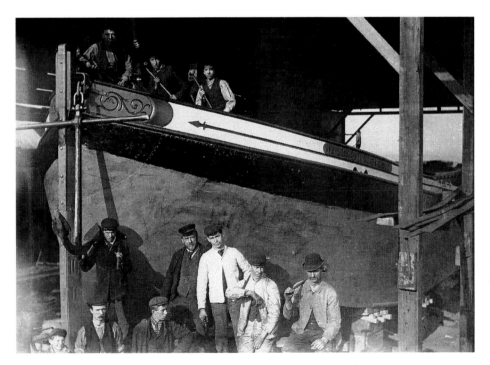

The Co-op yard at Borstal built barges for a number of local owners, including the Horsnaill family based in Canal Road. The yard staff and workforce gather for the photograph prior to the launch of the *William Cleverley,* their latest creation, on 11 March 1899.

A small boy in Corporation Street studies some hairy driving on the part of a Post Office employee, while one of Mr Brackley's big Austin taxis is followed by a motorcycle combination towards Star Hill. The driver of the Sheerness bus tries to stop the overtaking Austin by hand signal, something that was part of the Highway Code in those distant days.

Opposite: Ancient and modern are represented in this picture of the Norman west door of the cathedral which dates from the middle of the twelfth century. The brand-new car outside belongs to Mr Frith, a Rochester chemist, who has organised this photocall with his wife and daughter in about 1906.

For many years, a part of the castle moat was occupied by the yard of Messrs Trice's Garage and car hire business. More modern vehicles still use this area as a public car park.

In the 1930s, Rochester's fire station was to be found under some redundant railway arches on The Common, where the photographer has captured the chief fire officer posing in his new Singer 8, around 1934.

The inter-urban omnibus services were operated by Maidstone and District Motor Services Ltd from 1908 until nationalisation in 1974. This open-topped Leyland double-decker is an inter-war vehicle, with bodywork by Short Brothers of Rochester, and is posing for its official picture on the esplanade, around 1928.

Rochester's trams were withdrawn in 1930, being replaced by buses of the Chatham and District Traction Co. which had a distinctive brown and green livery. Here, a 1938 Bristol of the company pulls away from the Vineyard stop on its way to Borstal.

Left: Disruption caused by road maintenance is not a recent phenomenon. Here, the Improved Wood Pavement Co. of Blackfriars House, New Bridge Street, EC4, has taken over North Street and there will be no trams to Frindsbury for quite a while.

Below: Maidstone and District Motor Services absorbed the Chatham and District Traction Co., successors to the tram operators, in 1955. The penultimate Brown Bus VKO 998, new in 1955, has here been repainted in Maidstone and District green and passes the Three Gardeners in North Street on its way to the Wagon-at-Hale.

30 September 1930 was the last day of tram operation and scenes such as this, with two cars passing in Rochester's narrow High Street, would, within twelve hours, be history.

Above: The Chatham and District Light Railway Co. had been running trams in Chatham and Gillingham for six years before they extended the system to Rochester in 1908. Car No. 40 heads east for New Brampton (now Gillingham High Street) along an otherwise empty New Road, with the ivy-clad St Bartholomew's Hospital on the left.

The Trams in High Street, Strood.

The owner of the Austin Chummy on the right was out on 30 September 1930 to record the last day of tram operation, and has caught a Borstal-bound car on Priestfields. The conductor gazes at the receding scene, perhaps contemplating his work on the morrow with the new-fangled petrol buses. It is worth noting that the road known as Priestfields was, in 1930, still a relatively recent creation. It had been planned simply as a line of reserved track connecting the existing tramway on the main Rochester to Maidstone road to the village of Borstal, across former ecclesiastical land. However, it was constructed, in 1908, as a road and quickly became one of the city's more sought-after residential areas. Known at first as Priestfield Avenue, it assumed its current, shorter name - for reasons which are unclear - in 1927.

Opposite below: Another tram route through the city ran from the top of Strood Hill to Gillingham. Here Car No. 40, again Gillingham-bound, is about to pass St Nicholas' Church and will, very shortly, join up with yet another route, from Frindsbury.

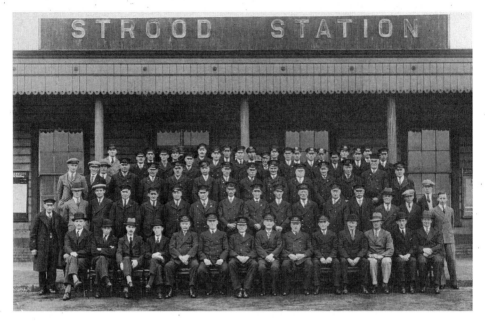

Sixty-eight of the staff of Rochester and Strood stations were gathered outside the latter for a group photograph in 1930. As well as management and platform staff, the group includes signalmen, shunters, carriage cleaners, and so on. Mr Fares, the stationmaster, is seated seventh from the left in the front row. On his right is Mr Washford, assistant stationmaster, later to become mayor of Rochester.

South Eastern and Chatham railway D class 4-4-0 locomotive No. 730 passes through Rochester Station in 1902 on a Ramsgate to Victoria express. Rochester Station was only ten years old then, having been opened in 1892, and within a further ten years was to be rebuilt as a four-road station. No. 730 was almost new when Ken Nunn took this picture on a sunny June day.

Rochester Station was rebuilt and resignalled in 1911, when loop tracks and two further platforms were installed. A locomotive of the M3 class, built by the London, Chatham and Dover railway, here runs in with a London-bound train. In 1899 the LCDR and its arch rival, the South Eastern railway, had formed a joint management committee, the combined operation becoming known as the South Eastern and Chatham Railway.

As well as being served by the London, Chatham and Dover Railway, Rochester was also served by a short branch of the South Eastern Railway from Strood. The line, barely a mile long, served an intermediate station at Rochester Common and a terminus named Chatham Central, although it stopped well short of the Chatham boundary. Here, rail motor No. 2 poses for its photograph at Chatham Central around 1905.

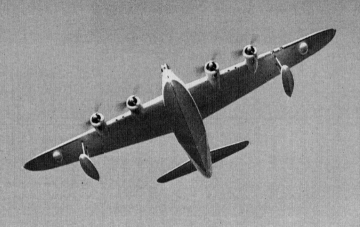

From 1914 to 1946 Rochester was closely involved in the British aircraft industry through the presence of the Short Bros' works on the esplanade and at the airport. Their products presented an awe-inspiring sight when flying low over the towns, and the roar of a Sunderland's four engines running up at Rochester could often be heard in Gillingham, three miles away.

Opposite above: The Short Bros' first factory buildings at Rochester were next to Churchfields, known also as Backfields. The corrugated iron sheds of 1914 were eventually replaced by purpose-built hangers as the size of the product increased. After Shorts departed, these buildings were taken over by other firms but they were all replaced by housing developments in the 1990s.

Opposite below: Here a 'Kent' flying boat is being lowered into the Medway, *c.*1930. Although the works have long gone, traces of the slipway down which the aircraft were launched can still be seen today.

Church Fields and Waterplane Works Rochester (878)

Short Brothers brought aircraft construction to the Medway from the Isle of Sheppey in 1914 and by the 1930s were pre-eminent in their field. The zenith of their commercial designs was the S23 Empire series of four-engine monoplanes. The prototype, *Canopus*, features here with the castle and cathedral in the background, in June 1936.

A larger version of the Empire was the G class, which was intended for the North Atlantic route. Here, *Golden Hind* thunders up the river on her take-off run, in the last days before the start of the Second World War. She was to return to the Medway in 1954, finally being wrecked in the Swale at Harty Ferry.

Shorts also built land-based planes which included the Stirling, the first of the heavy bombers of the Second World War. Though not as successful as the later Lancaster, they served throughout the war from 1941, latterly as glider tugs. The sight and sound of one landing at Rochester Airport was indeed memorable.

In the depression of the late 1920s Shorts built a wide variety of items to maintain employment for their workforce. These included bus bodies like this one for the East Kent Road Car Company, having its photograph taken in front of the gate to the castle gardens in 1926.

A major industry in the city from 1860 until 1932 was the road locomotive works of Aveling and Porter, sited on Strood Esplanade. Their office block, built to the design of local architect George E. Bond in 1910, is now part of the civic centre, as is the detached house on the left, which at one time was the home of Charles Dickens' doctor.

Road rollers were a major part of the Aveling and Porter production, with more being built at Strood than the sum total of all other companies combined. Numerous examples remain to carry the brass horse symbol, either in museums or as much-cared-for possessions of enthusiasts. They were exported worldwide, as this advertising card shows.

Glover's Mill was a fine smock mill dating from 1853. Also known as Delce Mill, it stood at the junction of Cossack Street and Longley Road until its demolition in the late 1940s. Although the mill itself did not quite reach its centenary, the base did as it lasted until the whole area was redeveloped in the 1960s.

Above: The mill at Star Hill was variously known as Boy's Mill or Belsey's Mill depending on the owner at the time. It was demolished in 1890-95 by Messrs Payne and Seymour, who had paid £50 for it! Today the building on the right is occupied by Rochester Independent College.

Left: The ridge of high land at Frindsbury boasted a number of mills in the nineteenth century. One stood at the junction of Bill Street Road and what is now Powlett Road, until it was demolished in 1929. Only the miller's house remains today. The back of this postcard records the precise time of demolition: 5.10 p.m. on 14 April.

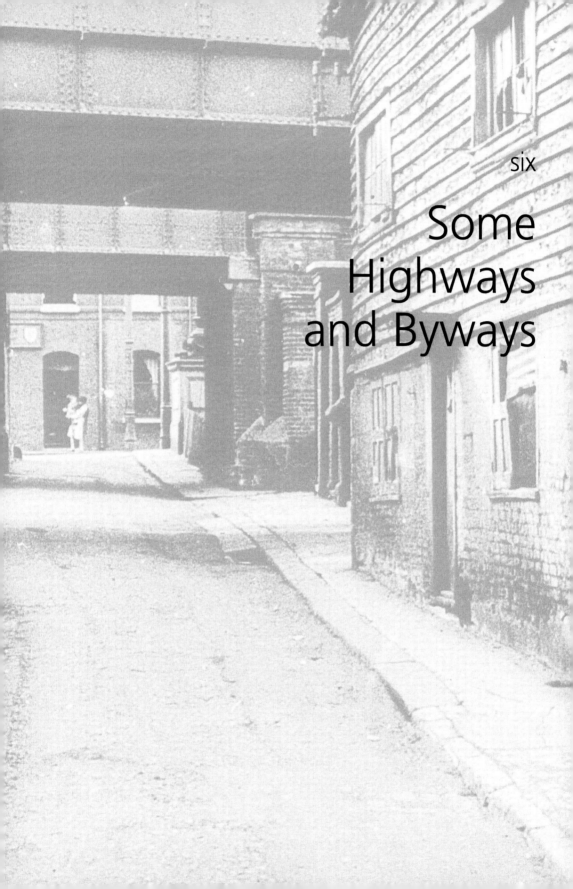

six

Some Highways and Byways

The Common was originally a byroad giving access to the river and to the riverside common land. Early in the twentieth century, it was transformed into Corporation Street, a major traffic thoroughfare linking Star Hill with Rochester Bridge, bypassing part of the High Street. Both roads carried two-way traffic until 1935 when Strood-bound traffic was confined to the High Street and Chatham-bound traffic to Corporation Street. Widened in the 1970s it now once again carries two-way traffic as part of the A2 route through the Medway towns. This early view of the western end of Corporation Street, looking towards the bridge and with the London, Chatham and Dover Railway viaduct on the right, shows some good examples of modes of transport of that era including two motor lorries, two steam traction engines and two horse-drawn delivery vans.

Opposite above: In this view from the '50s, a lone Maidstone and District bus on route No. 70 makes its way towards Chatham from Upnor, while the (free) car park on the right is occupied by an Austin van and two cars. Look closely and note the only other traffic: six cyclists. On the left is the corrugated iron building which once covered part of the cattle market.

Opposite below: Four of Rochester's youth appear oblivious to the traffic at the Corporation Street junction with High Street on a summer Saturday in the late 1950s. The ex-army Bedford was owned by H.J. Taylors, a local vegetable wholesaler. The Red Lion public house and Clift & Co. pawnbrokers, at No. 179 High Street, have since gone in a road-widening scheme that has made this view unrecognisable today. Contrast this view with those on pages 52 and 122.

Above: Corporation Street lies to the left of this composite view of Rochester Cattle Market, with Davis Square beyond and the main line of the London, Chatham and Dover Railway on the right. Before the coming of the railway this area was open to the river, away to the right, and was mainly common land used for the grazing of cattle. Over the centuries, markets had been held in various locations of the city and the general market followed the cattle market in establishing itself here in the nineteenth century. The cattle market ceased in the 1960s. A general market and a farmers' market continue to be held here at the time of writing, although redevelopment plans for the area mean that they may be moved elsewhere in the near future. The large building looming over the rooftops on the left is the new corn exchange. Opened in 1871, the design of its principal room, the Queen's Hall, was influenced by the banqueting hall of the Cutlers' Co. in Sheffield.

Opposite below: A view of the cattle market in the early years of the twentieth century. The market was held on Tuesdays, when the farming community from the surrounding area would bring their stock to the pens in Corporation Street for sale, often driving them on foot through the streets of the city. Considerable activity is seen here in progress, to be no doubt followed by further gatherings in the High Street hostelries.

Above: Weekends brought major traffic congestion to Rochester in the days before the opening of the M2 motorway. Two lorries of Messrs Bourne and Hillier, the local milk distribution company, vie with a coast-bound coach as they approach the junction at the bottom of Star Hill. Bourne and Hillier's office and main distribution depot were in the buildings on the left of the picture.

Below: Bardell Terrace, at the end of Corporation Street, was the home of Post Office vans. The Morris Commercial and its little friend on the left are in the dark-green livery of the 'Telephones', while the Morris 8 mail vans on the right wear pillar box red. These vans also had rubber mudguards. In the background, a Kentish coal train heads for London.

Above and below: An Act of Parliament in 1768 authorised the construction of a new road bypassing the High Streets of Rochester and Chatham. Even now, nearly 240 years later, it is still known as New Road. Land on its north side was gradually developed, including, in 1863, a new building for St Bartholomew's Hospital *(above).* However, the War Department owned the land to the south and today it is public recreation grounds. Charles Dickens found difficulty in determining where Rochester ends and Chatham begins. The view below illustrates his point: the sheep in the foreground are grazing in Rochester while the houses below sit just across the boundary in Chatham. The question has been largely academic since 1974, however, when city and borough were brought together under a single local authority. Part of Chatham Dockyard can be seen in the left background.

Early in the nineteenth century the defences of Chatham and Rochester were strengthened by the construction of a new chain of forts encircling the towns. Rochester's Fort Clarence consisted of a central tower, in Borstal Road, to which guardhouses were joined by fortified ditches. While the central tower remains today, converted into flats, the outlying guardhouses have been demolished. The Medway Tower, on the riverbank, was demolished to make way for the expansion of Short Brothers' aircraft works. The remains of the Maidstone Road guard house, however, seen in this early twentieth-century view, lingered on until they were demolished in 1965, the land having been acquired for a depot for British Telecom.

Opposite: At one time a terrace of houses at the top of Boley Hill - home to members of Rochester's Quaker community - blocked the view of the castle from St Margaret's Street. The terrace is here seen being demolished in the 1950s. Its removal opened up a view of the castle that is today much appreciated by photographers.

Bishopscourt, at the junction of St Margaret's Street and Vines Lane, became home to the bishops of Rochester in 1922, although it was originally bequeathed for episcopal use as early as 1674. The interesting pattern of rendering on a stone base, shown here, was removed during renovation in the 1920s. The house gained its present name when the bishop took up residence; it had previously been known as The Old Palace.

The Cooper's Arms, at the corner of Love Lane and St Margaret's Street, is said to be Rochester's oldest public house. It survives today, a gem hidden from the route of the general tourist, though the little cottage next door, depicted in this nineteenth-century view, has been demolished. Perhaps the stock of people small enough to live there dried up.

It is difficult today to imagine that there was once a row of houses in the castle moat. Some were still standing when this shot was taken in the early 1960s but the 'sold' board suggests that, for one at least, the end was nigh. The right-hand end of the terrace marks the edge of the 'little graveyard under the castle wall', where Charles Dickens wished to be buried.

Number 28 St Margaret's Street once fronted a maltings. After a further life as a printer's store this was demolished in the 1980s and replaced by housing known as Malt Mews. The original street elevation is seen here. During the demolition the partial frame of an ancient timber barn was discovered within the brick structure.

Left and below: The Roebuck *(left)* was another small public house in St Margaret's Street, at the corner of Roebuck Lane (later Roebuck Road). It was rebuilt at the turn of the twentieth century and survived as a public house until the early 1990s *(below)*, when it was converted for residential use. Canon Sydney Wheatley, a vicar of nearby St Margaret's church and one of the city's most celebrated historians, conjectured that the name Roebuck was inspired by one of the heraldic devices which once adorned the medieval bridge. St Margaret's Street is one of the oldest of the city's thoroughfares. It forms part of an ancient route which runs, roughly parallel with the river, towards Aylesford and Maidstone. Originally very narrow (it still is in places), it has been widened here and there and nineteenth- and twentieth-century villas have taken the place of its old wooden cottages.

The cameraman is here looking south along St Margaret's Street with the churchyard wall on the right, before the road was widened and Whiston's cottages were replaced by the houses in the next picture. To the left of the cottages can be seen some of the (then new) villas in Watts Avenue.

The late nineteenth and early twentieth centuries saw rows of substantial villas spring up in this part of the city, many to be occupied by naval and military personnel and their families. These two, opposite St Margaret's church, were built around 1900. The rest-gate at the entrance to the churchyard, on the extreme left of the picture, was erected in 1932 in memory of Mr Charles Arnott, a former parishioner.

Left: As late as the 1960s most side streets in Rochester were still lit by gas lamps such as this one at the corner of Thomas Street and Cossack Street. The house to the right is one of a row which was provided in the late nineteenth century for employees of the South Eastern Railway. Unlike many in this part of the city, these houses were spared the attentions of the bulldozers and are with us today.

Below: Cazeneuve Street and East Row are in Troy Town, an area close to the city centre which was developed in the late eighteenth century on land owned by John Cazeneuve Troy, a Chatham wine merchant. When this photograph was taken in the 1950s the houses here were approaching the end of their days. They were shortly to be demolished to make way for Rochester's new police station.

Above: To the south of Troy Town lies the Delce, taking its name from its main artery, Delce Road. Formerly a farming and market gardening area, it was developed in the nineteenth and early twentieth centuries with mainly small, terraced houses, many of which were swept away in the 1960s and '70s. Here, two aspiring footballers practice their game in a traffic-free Rose Street.

Right: A study in concentration, as two young men watch their friend trace patterns in a puddle. The place is Cross Street, one of the network of narrow streets in the Delce. The houses in the right background are in Castle Avenue. Cross Street was one of those which, in the late 1960s, would be swept away in the slum-clearance programme.

Above and below: Borstal was a hamlet which became joined to Rochester in the nineteenth century by ribbon development along Borstal Road. It also gave its name to the pioneering corrective institute for young offenders, first mooted in 1902 and thereafter established here. The novelty of the tramway, newly laid into the village, is evident in the attention which car No. 24 is receiving from a group of young residents *(above)*. By 1934, when the photograph below was taken, buses had replaced the trams and one of the Chatham and District Traction Company's vehicles approaches the end of its run on route No. 5 from Gillingham Strand.

Right and below: Bull Lane *(right)* and George Lane *(below)* were two of a number of lanes, courts and alleys which ran north from the High Street towards The Common and the river. The coming of the railways in the nineteenth century severed these ancient byways and obliterated many buildings, including the last vestiges of the ancient parish church of St Clement. The effect was to create what Charles Dickens described, in *Edwin Drood*, as a number of 'disappointing yards with pumps in them and no thoroughfare'. These two photographs were taken as part of the submission for an Act of Parliament in 1903 which authorised the laying out of Corporation Street, and they bear labels recording this fact.

ROCHESTER CASTLE P.H

George Lane.

5 0

Left: Horsewash Lane is another of the narrow thoroughfares which leads away from the High Street. It was bridged by the two railway lines serving Rochester at the turn of the twentieth century. Both companies' bridges can be seen in this view. The South Eastern Railway is closest and the London, Chatham and Dover furthest from the camera. The former remains today, but all the surrounding structures have long gone.

Below: The forts guarding the towns were strategically placed at their main entry points. Gated archways ensured that access could be prevented in times of trouble. Here, Fort Clarence straddles the road leading out of the city through Borstal. In later years the arch became an obstruction to the movement of traffic and was demolished, amid some controversy, in 1924. The guardhouse at the east end of the Fort Clarence complex, in Maidstone Road, can be seen on p.88.

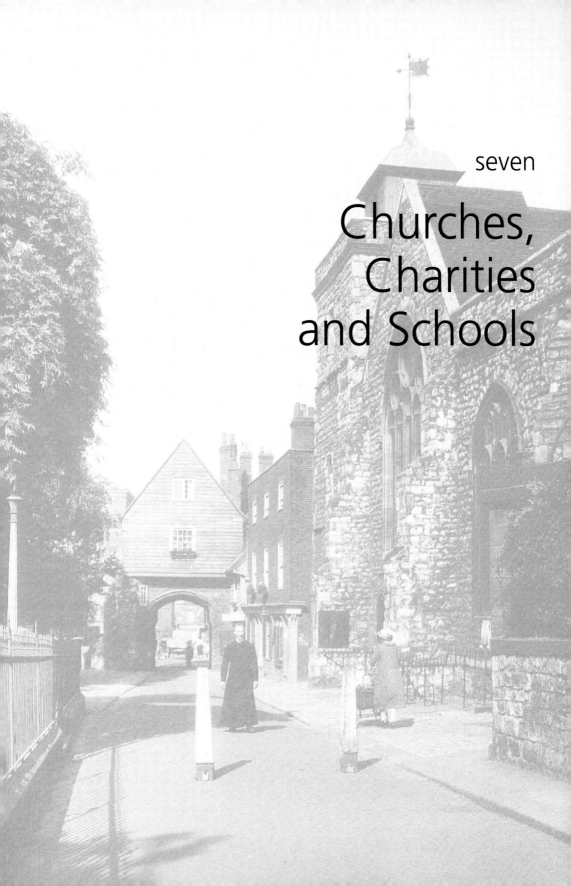

seven

Churches, Charities and Schools

About half a mile south of the city centre lies St Margaret's church. Built to serve a mainly rural parish, the growing population in nineteenth-century Rochester resulted in the rebuilding of the medieval nave and chancel between 1823 and 1840, though the old tower was retained. In common with many other churches, burials in the churchyard have long since ceased and the gravestones have now been set back against the wall.

St Peter's church, King Street. By the middle of the nineteenth century, Rochester's population had grown to the point where it was necessary to create a separate parish to serve the eastern part of the city. The parish church was built in 1859 in the decorated Gothic style to the design of the aptly named Mr Ewan Christian, and could accommodate 880 worshippers. It was demolished in 1974, being replaced by a new church in Delce Road, and the site is now occupied by a block of flats. In 1953 the wheel turned full circle and the two parishes were once again combined.

Above and right: In the shadow of the
cathedral stands the old church of St
Nicholas, once the parish church of central
Rochester. It was built in 1423 and rebuilt
in the seventeenth century. In 1961 its parish
was combined with that of St Peter and St
Margarets, and St Nicholas was converted for
use as offices by the diocese of Rochester.
The view of the interior *(above)* shows the
galleries which had been inserted above the
north and south aisles to accommodate what
must have been a very large congregation.
The exterior view *(right)* was taken before
railings were removed to support the war
effort.

The choir and others holding office in St Nicholas' church pose for the official photograph in 1919. The vicar, Canon William Gray, is seated fifth from the left in the second row. Ernest Moss, father of one of the authors, is second from the left in the front row.

The Baptist church in Crow Lane was designed by local architect George E. Bond and built in 1912. The handsome lamp hanging above the main entrance in this early view has sadly disappeared. The building was later embellished with a plaque on the right hand turret commemorating the Protestant Martyrs of Kent of the sixteenth century.

The Chatham Memorial Synagogue is actually in Rochester High Street, albeit a very short distance from the meeting point of the two towns. It was built in 1868 by Simon Magnus following the death of his son. A house was also provided for the Rabbi, although this has since been demolished and replaced by an assembly hall. Both house and synagogue can here be seen in this Edwardian photograph. The little graveyard behind contains some interesting memorials, including one to Daniel Barnard, founder of two of Chatham's theatres, Barnard's Palace of Varieties and Theatre Royal.

Strood. *The New Cemetery.*

The Wrench Series, No. 9714

The city had two parish churches dedicated to St Nicholas, in Rochester and in Strood. This view shows St Nicholas' Strood around the turn of the twentieth century. The dedication to the patron saint of fishermen is especially apt here, given that Strood has been home to generations of Medway fishermen. As with St Margaret's, the medieval building was demolished leaving just the tower, to which a new nave and chancel were added in 1812. To the benefit of the fabric, the considerable covering of ivy apparent in this view was later stripped away.

Opposite above: Strood Methodist church, at the corner of Frindsbury Road and Cliffe Road, was opened in 1887. It cost £5,700 and had seating capacity for 700. In 1899 the Wesley hall, to the left in this view of the church, was added at a further cost of £1,650. The church itself was demolished in 1970 leaving the hall to serve as the meeting place for the Methodist congregation.

Opposite below: Strood Cemetery in Cuxton Road was opened in 1883 as St Nicholas' parish churchyard had by then nearly reached its capacity. As was customary at that time, two chapels were provided, one for Anglicans and one for Nonconformists. The cemetery occupies high ground overlooking the city and the Medway, a view which had earlier been painted by J.M.W. Turner.

Above: Rochester can boast one of the first grammar schools for girls in the country. At a time when the education of young women was still given low priority, the Rochester Bridge Trust provided the finance to enable construction to proceed and this pioneering establishment was opened on 22 January 1889. The school vacated this building in 1990 and the site was redeveloped for housing shortly afterwards. In this photograph the tramlines appear to still be in situ although the overhead wires have gone, suggesting a date in the early 1930s.

Below: In the 1890s Rochester Corporation added a new wing to the guildhall to be used for 'Art, Science and Technical Schools and Classes'. However, it appears not to have been ideal for the purpose and a wholly new building, erected on a site near Eastgate House, had been completed by 1907. This fine building still exists today, though with some less meritorious extensions. It now houses the City Adult Education Centre.

Above and below: Rochester's public school is King's School, known as the Grammar School in the nineteenth century. The main part of the school *(above)* was built in 1842 but had already been extended by 1900 when this photograph was taken. It still survives today, although it is buried in further extensions. Given a new charter by King Henry VIII during the Reformation, King's School is Rochester's oldest educational establishment, and claims to have been founded, with the cathedral, by Bishop Justus in AD 604. To accommodate an increasing number of pupils a new boarding house *(below)* was erected in 1880. Restoration House can also be glimpsed in the background of this late nineteenth-century view across The Vines.

The Mathematical School was founded in 1708 for the education of the sons of Freemen of the City, under the terms of a bequest by Sir Joseph Williamson, a president of the Royal Society, secretary of state to King William III, and MP for Rochester. Here it is as it appeared after enlargement in 1882 but before the major rebuild of 1894.

The school opened in 1709, was enlarged in 1882 and rebuilt in 1894 by George E. Bond. C Block, in Free School Lane to the right, was added in 1912, again by Bond. The building is seen in its final form in this view from the 1950s. The school subsequently moved to new premises and the High Street site was cleared in 1969 revealing a substantial length of the old city wall which had long been hidden from view.

This view from 1956 shows the close juxtaposition of school and passing traffic, in the days when the High Street was still part of the A2 trunk road. The school had already acquired land about a mile to the south of the city, which was used as playing fields, and it was to this site that the whole school was eventually relocated.

Sir Joseph Williamson's intention was that the sons of Freemen of the City should be schooled in 'Mathematics and all other things which might fit and encourage them for the sea service and arts and callings leading and relating thereto'. This view of the art room leads one to wonder how much inspiration early twentieth-century pupils gained from their rather dreary surroundings.

Seven Poor Travellers' Rest, Rochester

A large oil lamp marks the entrance to the Poor Travellers' House, which was endowed under the will of Richard Watts in 1579 to give a night's lodging to six itinerant workmen. The house no longer provides that service but the charity remains active, caring for the elderly in a large almshouse complex in Maidstone Road. Charles Dickens wrote a short story about the house, calling it *The Seven Poor Travellers*, he being the seventh.

A group of travellers arrive to take up Mr Watts' beneficence. They would be given a meal, a bed for the night, breakfast and four old pence to go on their way. In 1934 the allowance was raised to one shilling (5p). The house closed in 1940 due to wartime restrictions and was not reopened to poor travellers after the war. It has since been restored and opened as a museum in memory of Richard Watts.

In the days when poor travellers still came to the house, it was the custom for some of them to go to the cathedral and lay a wreath on Richard Watts' grave on the anniversary of his death. The ceremony is here seen in progress, *c*. 1930.

In 1858, Watts' charity built almshouses for elderly residents of the city in Maidstone Road. The main building, of striking appearance, proved somewhat controversial when first completed. The very ornate arches above the gates were later removed. The almshouses were designed for twenty people, including nursing staff, but in recent years that number has considerably increased by the provision of additional units, some newly built and some in a large adjoining house.

The Foord Almshouses, Rochester.

Above and left: A bequest from Thomas Hellyar Foord, scion of a local shipbuilding family, enabled the building of this large complex of almshouses on an elevated site in Priestfields, about a mile from the centre of the city. It was designed to accommodate ten couples and thirty-seven single people, though this number was increased with later additions. It was formally opened on 28 June 1927 by Prince and Princess Arthur of Connaught.

Right: St Bartholomew's Hospital was founded by Bishop Gundulph in 1078. The present main building dates from 1863 but the chapel which formed part of the original leper hospital remains and is here pictured after restoration by Sir George Gilbert Scott in 1896. In 2006, the chapel faces an uncertain future having been declared redundant and sold by the health authority.

St Catherine's Almshouse was founded by Symond Potyn, landlord of the Crown Inn, in 1316. It was established in its present position at the top of Star Hill – then on the very outskirts of the city – in 1805. In this early photograph, City Way, which now joins Star Hill at this point, did not exist. The narrow thoroughfare in the foreground is the northern end of Patten's Lane. St Catherine's is now administered by the Richard Watts charity.

Theobald Square was built in 1840 on the site, off the High Street, of an old brewery. Seen here around the turn of the twentieth century it was then graced by a statue of the Duke of Sussex, a son of King George III. By 1960 the houses were in a very rundown condition, but in that year they were purchased by the Huguenot Society who renamed the square La Providence and converted the houses into sheltered accommodation for people of Huguenot descent.

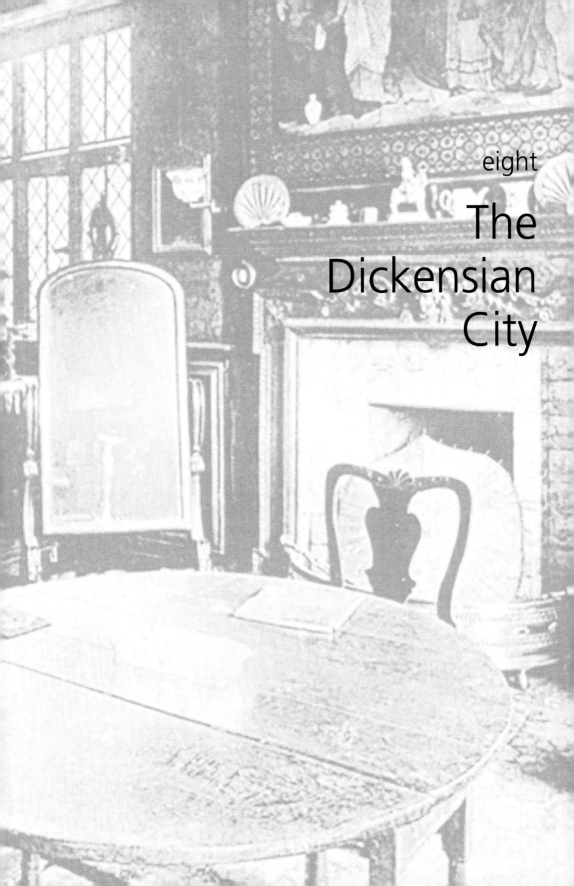

eight

The Dickensian City

Eastgate House is one of Rochester's landmark buildings. It had been built as a private dwelling during the late sixteenth and early seventeenth centuries but was in use as a school in the mid-nineteenth century. Indeed, Charles Dickens used it as the model for Miss Twinkleton's academy for young ladies in *Edwin Drood*. This rare, and sadly damaged, photograph shows the house at the end of the nineteenth century before its conversion into a museum. No trace now remains of the doorway and large windows on the ground floor street frontage.

Above and below: Eastgate House was also a young men's hostel and a temperance restaurant, before becoming the city's museum in 1903, and the Charles Dickens centre in 1979. The late Victorian view *(above)* shows the high wall and gates which held the outside world at bay when it was still in private ownership. The wall had gone and the house was welcoming visitors when the photograph *(below)* was taken soon after the opening of the museum. The modest fence was later replaced by a fine set of iron railings, which it retains. The right-hand chimney stack had also been made more in keeping with the period of the house. The Dickens centre closed in 2004 and, at the time of writing, the council is considering proposals to turn it into a literary centre.

Above: Another of Rochester's houses made famous (or more famous) by Charles Dickens is Restoration House in Crow Lane. Taking its name from the occasion in 1660 when King Charles II rested here en route to his own restoration to the throne, Dickens saw it as Satis House, the home of Miss Havisham in *Great Expectations.* This view was taken before the land in the foreground was more formally laid out as The Vines, in the 1880s.

Below: Sent from Maidstone to Lincoln in 1909, this postcard shows the room in which the King is reputed to have slept. Stephen Aveling, a nineteenth-century owner, painted the panels depicting scenes from the Arthurian legends which can be seen above the bed and fireplace. The house is once again a private dwelling but, together with its magnificent gardens, is open to the public at certain times.

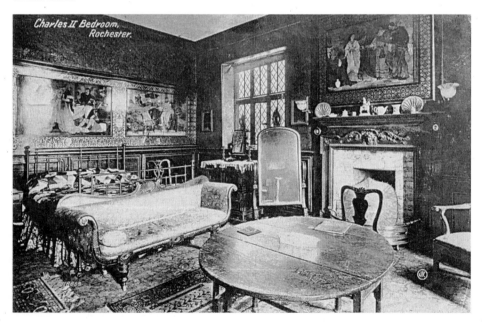

Above and below: It is said that the monks of St Andrew's priory had a vineyard hereabouts, which gives the area its name: The Vines. In this 1880s view *(above),* the saplings which were to form the avenue of plane trees have only just been planted and the area looks strangely bare. In the later view *(below),* taken around 1914 from the first floor of The Vineyard public house at the corner of Maidstone Road and East Row, the trees are maturing nicely and the cathedral has regained its spire. In Dickens's novel *The Mystery of Edwin Drood* it is here in the Monks' vineyard that the young Edwin encounters the old opium addict curiously nicknamed Princess Puffer.

The streets surrounding the cathedral are known as the Precincts and contain some large houses once occupied by the canons of the cathedral. MacKean House was built in 1840 and is named after the last canon to live there. It is now part of the King's School and its once extensive gardens have been developed with more housing.

The cathedral, its people and its Precincts feature significantly in *Edwin Drood*. Minor Canon Row (Minor Canon Corner in the novel) was home to the Revd Septimus Crisparkle and his elderly mother. On the south side, the eighteenth-century terrace in which they lived still stands but, on the north side, a fine eighteenth-century house and stables, of which this is the only known photograph, was demolished in 1887.

nine

People, Pubs and Pleasure

Local brewers Charles Arkoll owned the Red Lion on the corner of High Street and Ironmonger Lane, now Corporation Street. Road widening necessitated its rebuilding in 1904 and its successor, seen on p.83, was to last a further seventy years before it too succumbed to the needs of the motor car. Note the superb plasterwork around the door and the etched glass lions in the windows.

Mr Rose's Ship Inn stood at the west end of Rochester Bridge until the site was acquired in the early 1900s for the offices of Aveling and Porter, a picture of which is to be found on p.78. The offices today form part of the civic centre of the Medway unitary authority. Winch was a Chatham brewer, eventually joining with Style to form a well-known brewing firm based in Maidstone.

It is 11 August 1921 and the regulars of the Cooper's Arms in St Margaret's Street (see also p.90) are off to cricket at Canterbury. It would be interesting to know how long the journey took. There are some steep hills on the old road which might have proven quite a challenge for their little charabanc.

The heyday of the Bull Hotel, or The Royal Victoria and Bull Hotel to give it its current title, was as a resting place for travellers on the coach route from London to Canterbury and Dover. As such it was immortalised by Charles Dickens in *Pickwick Papers*. This view was taken in 1902 as it sports a large E and R at first floor level, in recognition of the coronation of King Edward VII in that year.

Most cities and larger boroughs had their own constabularies until they became subsumed into larger county forces. Here, on 14 June 1934, and nearing the end of their independent existence, the men of the City of Rochester Constabulary are on parade in the castle gardens for a visit by a government inspector. The force would soon become part of the Kent County Constabulary, based in Maidstone.

Beating the bounds is an activity normally associated with rural parishes, but these solemn gentlemen are beating the bounds of St Nicholas' Parish in the centre of Rochester on 29 June 1908. At this point, in Crow Lane, the boundary of St Nicholas met that of St Margaret. The two parishes, and that of St Peter, have since been combined and the tradition of beating the bounds has been revived.

The former Liberal Club in Castle Hill was transformed into the Castle Theatre in 1931 and was home to Rochester's own repertory company for the next seven years. The opening production, on 7 December 1931, was *To Have The Honour*, a play written by A.A. Milne. After it ceased to be used as a theatre the building took on yet another lease of life, as Rochester's police station. It was demolished in 1975 and the site is now a car park

The Theatre Royal on Star Hill was opened in the late eighteenth century by Mrs Sarah Baker, who owned theatres in a number of Kentish towns. The young Charles Dickens is said to have paid his first visit to the theatre here. The Theatre Royal closed its doors for the last time on 12 April 1884 and was replaced by the Conservative Club, now the Royal Function Rooms.

In 1924 the New Medway Steam Packet Co. took delivery of *Medway Queen*, the latest addition to their fleet and built for them by the Ailsa Shipbuilding Co. of Troon. She is pictured arriving at Strood Pier on return from a day trip to the Kent coast. It is 1963 and she is very near the end of her active life. At the time of writing, she lies in a creek on the lower Medway where valiant efforts are still being made to preserve her. *Medway Queen* was one of the most famous of the flotilla of little ships which rescued our troops from the beaches at Dunkirk in 1940. In 2006, it is still possible to enjoy a trip on a paddle steamer down the Medway, for the *Kingswear Castle* operates a regular service in the summer months.

Opposite: A typical handbill of the New Medway Steam Packet Co., from their last season of operation. Between the two world wars the Rochester-based company owned a fleet of large (but mostly second-hand) paddle steamers, known as the Queen Line of Steamers. They plied the Medway and Thames Estuary and ranged as far afield as Great Yarmouth and Boulogne.

QUEEN LINE STEAMERS

1963 SEASON SUMMER CRUISES

by p.s. "MEDWAY QUEEN"

Daily (except Fridays)

on the RIVER MEDWAY and THAMES ESTUARY

(Vessel available for charter by large parties)

Commencing Saturday, 1st June, 1963

Every Saturday

TWO SAILINGS TO SOUTHEND

Depart STROOD	9.30 a.m.
Arrive SOUTHEND	11.10 a.m.
Depart SOUTHEND	11.30 a.m.
Arrive STROOD	1.10 p.m.

Depart STROOD	4.15 p.m.
Arrive SOUTHEND	5.55 p.m.
(NON-LANDING)	
Depart SOUTHEND	6.15 p.m.
Arrive STROOD	7.55 p.m.

Every Monday and Wednesday

TO SOUTHEND & CLACTON

Depart STROOD	9.15 a.m.
„ SOUTHEND	11.00 a.m.
Arrive CLACTON	1.25 p.m.

Depart CLACTON	2.45 p.m.
(SEA TRIP)	
Arrive CLACTON	4.15 p.m.

Depart CLACTON	4.25 p.m.
„ SOUTHEND	6.40 p.m.
Arrive STROOD	8.40 p.m.

Every Sunday, Tuesday and Thursday

TO SOUTHEND & HERNE BAY

Depart STROOD	9.15 a.m.
„ SOUTHEND	11.00 a.m.
„ HERNE BAY	12.30 p.m.
Arrive SOUTHEND	2.15 p.m.

Depart SOUTHEND	3.15 p.m.
„ HERNE BAY	5.00 p.m.
„ SOUTHEND	6.40 p.m.
Arrive STROOD	8.40 p.m.

FARES FROM STROOD

			SINGLE		DAY RETURN	PERIOD
TO	**SOUTHEND**	Sun., Mon., Tues., Wed. and Thurs.	7/-	approx. 7½ hrs. ashore	10/-	12/6
„	**SOUTHEND**	Saturdays (Non-Landing 7/6)		approx. 7 hrs. ashore	10/-	
TO	**HERNE BAY**	Sundays, Tuesdays and Thursdays	7/6	approx. 4½ hrs. ashore	11/-	12/6
„	**CLACTON**	Mondays and Wednesdays	10/6	approx. 3 hrs. ashore	14/-	18/6
„	**MARGATE**	Daily (except Fridays)	12/-	approx. 2 hrs. ashore	15/-	20/-

(CHANGE AT SOUTHEND)

Children under 14 half fare. Under 3 free.
Luggage allowed to Single and Period Passengers only.
Bicycles 5/- single.
Fully Licensed Bars.
Attractive Meals and Refreshments served (May be booked in advance)
Special Rates for Parties of 20 and over.
Ample parking facilities adjacent to Pier.
All Sailings are subject to weather and other circumstances permitting.
No dogs allowed on board.

Further Particulars and Bookings :—

THE NEW MEDWAY STEAM PACKET

CO., LTD.,

GAS HOUSE ROAD, ROCHESTER

Telephone: Chatham 41355-6-7

For Conditions of Carriage see over

Other local titles published by The History Press

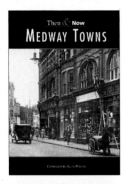

Medway Towns Then & Now
ALUN PEDLER

The area collectively known as the Medway Towns –Strood, Rochester, Chatham and Gillingham – has seen an unprecedented rate of change in the last hundred years. This fascinating collection of around ninety pairs of old and new photographs tells the story of this development. Throughout this collection the photographs are accompanied by interesting and informative captions containing a wealth of detail.

0 7524 1623 5

Voices of Kent and East Sussex Hop Pickers
HILARY HEFFERNAN

Right up to the late 1950s, the annual hop-picking season provided a welcome escape for thousands of families who lived and worked in the poorer parts of London, who would migrate every year to the hop gardens of Kent and Sussex to pick the harvest. The photographs and reminiscences in this book tell a fascinating story; of hardship, adventures, mishaps, misfortune and laughter experienced during hardworking holidays among the bines.

0 7524 3240 0

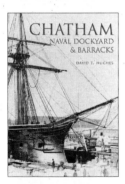

Chatham Naval Dockyard
DAVID HUGHES

This is a thoughtful volume of photographs and ephemera on the Chatham Naval Dockyard and Barracks, looking at it from its early days of existence until its role in more recent years, from the First and Second World Wars to the Falklands.

0 7524 3248 6

Folklore of Kent
FRAN AND GEOFF DOEL

Kentish folklore reflects the curious geography and administrative history of Kent, with its extensive coastline and strong regional differences between east and west reflected in its distinctive cultural traditions. The authors explore the folklore, legends, customs and songs of Kent and the causative factors underlying them.

0 7524 2628 6

If you are interested in purchasing other books published by The History Press, or in case you have difficulty finding any of our books in your local bookshop, you can also place orders directly through our website
www.thehistorypress.co.uk